John Ngong Kum Ngong

THE TEETH OF TIME

And Other Poems

Miraclaire Publishing
Kansas City (MO) / Yaounde

MIRACLAIRE PUBLISHING LLC
Kansas City (MO), USA

Website: *www.miraclairepublishing.com*
Email: *info@miraclairepublishing.com*

P.O. Box 8616
Yaounde, Cameroon

ISBN-13: 978-0615957692
ISBN-10: 0615957692

All rights reserved.
No part of this publication may be reproduced by any means, graphic, electronic, or mechanical, including photocopying, recording, taping or by any information storage retrieval system without the prior written permission of the copyright holder, except in the case of brief quotations embodied in critical articles and reviews.

© 2014 Miraclaire Publishing
John Ngong Kum Ngong

Printed in the United States of America

Miraclaire Publishing makes every effort to ensure the accuracy of all the information ("Content") in its publications. However, Miraclaire and its agents and licensors make no representations or warranties whatsoever as to the accuracy, completeness, or suitability for any purpose of the Content and disclaim all such representations and warranties, whether expressed or implied to the maximum extent permitted by law. Any views expressed in this publication are the views of the author and are not necessarily the views of Miraclaire.

CONTENTS

THE TEETH OF TIME	5
WATCHDOG	8
WAKE UP	11
DO SOMETHING SANE	13
SMALL MINDS	15
GROOM OUR IMAGE	17
I WILL DO MY BEST	19
KEEPING DISTANCE TO MOULD	21
YEARS GONE BY	23
SPITEFUL CONSCIENCE	25
TIRED AND SICK	27
MOKOLO ELOBI	29
THE FACE I WANT	31
RUNNING WITH PATIENCE	33
HEAVY HANDED	35
CONTEMPTUOUS	37
DEPLOY YOUR BRAINS	39
ON THE VERGE OF SIXTY	41
COME OUT	44
EMPATHY	46
COCKS NO LONGER CROW	48
RAGE IN HANDCUFFS	50
POISON IN MY BLOOD	52
HEART IN BLACK	54
LEARNED MEN IN GREY	56
IGNOMINY	58
STATUS QUO	59
NIGHTMARE OF LIFE	61
CONTENT WITH MY ME	62
STARTING POINT	64
WRITE A NEW STORY	66
ALWAYS CALL TO MIND	68

VARNISHED WITH THE SAME BRUSH	70
TWO VOICES	72
SEEKING A NEW IMAGE	73
MISCONSTRUED POET	75
TAKE OFF YOUR MASK	77
RISK OF RUST	79
THERE WILL BE LIGHT AGAIN	81
SHAMELESS SILENCE	83
BRED ON LORE	85
I CANNOT RESTRAIN MYSELF	87
I DOFF MY CAP	89
INCENSE OF HOME	91
SHROUDED IN MIST	93
THE LAND LIES LIFELESS	95
BAD BLOOD	96
A NEW DAWN IN GESTATION	98

THE TEETH OF TIME

1
The iron teeth of time
will never cut a deal
with finite flesh and blood
whether black or yellow
or caucasian or brown
nor negotiate with earth,
the mate of corrupt flesh.

Stash away all the gold
and the silver you can
in lands beyond the sea
or in holes in the ground
but do not forget that
the steely teeth of time
and time have the last word.

Feed your ambition well
sleeping on human hide
and agree with your greed
to grind the hard up down
but do not forget that
you cannot outwit time
nor break the teeth of time.

Time burns away the rich
as well as those in rags
and tears both the pretty
and the ugly like flesh.
The teeth of time are sharp
and often give full vent
to their fits of temper.

2
You and I countrymen
like the rest of mankind
can neither take up arms
nor conceive a sound scheme
to dodge the teeth of time.
You and I fellow poets
cannot bind time either.

If time were but clement
and the teeth of time blunt
man would lose sight of God
and become his own man.
Small minds would strip the fields
and turn their backs on love,
all out to rule the roost.

The canine teeth of time
will never put up with
red tape and lazybones
nor tolerate the whims
and the hubris of man
bending over backwards
in a bid to boss time.

I know time works a cure
for those with running sores
and kills at the same time
when its poisonous fangs
sink deep into our flesh.
We cannot conquer time
but we can wrestle well

while time is ours to use
and die well crossing swords
with life so hard so fierce.
The teeth of time, bitchy
and greedy as male dogs
wait in silence and hope
to grind the world save God.

WATCHDOG

I do not compose
hallelujah songs
nor back like a bat
the deeds of people
blinded by self-praise,
people who drown dreams
and drug daring poets.

I do not compose
propaganda songs
nor close my egg eyes
to the fat maggots
and the deadly worms
crawling in our streets,
searching for new game.

You cannot pretend
not to see the mess
and the blood of maids
flowing down bone slabs
in the heart of town
swamped by racketeers
and riddled with crime.

I am the watchdog
of my abused clan
barking day and night
while you laugh and boast
basking in our gold,
unmoved by the tears

of a bleeding breed.

I will not stick to
barking and wailing
like a toothless dog.
Someday for certain
I shall sink my teeth
deep into your flesh
grasping countrymen
if you do not let
me and my people
savour our wealth too.

I will join the crowd
to end our sad tale
of planting in tears
and harvesting blood.
I am convinced that
ere my time to go
and show the whole world
we count and matter
though we plant in tears,
burdened by dashed hopes.
I am convinced that
ere my time to go
the matchete of time
and poetic justice
would wreck wickedness
and silence tin gods.
For the time being
my me and my head

have to kill dear time
licking into shape
my mind and senses,
glad to be watchdog
of my abused clan
barking set to bite
till time sinks its teeth
into my frail flesh.

WAKE UP

If my style sickens you
just like light and conscience
disconcert corrupt minds,
lower your king size head
and find out from yourself
whether you are not nuts
before time caves you in.

You pull my leg all day
and pee on all my songs
just like little minds do.
You run through me with hate
and hawk my eyes to hawks
to seize all that I own
but you will sink someday
green with envy scoundrel
when time tears you apart.

You slander me daily
with quacks on your payroll
and tear my poems in rage
with the demons round you.
You seem to forget sirs
that someday for certain
just as blooms bloom and die
and time exacts a toll
you will sleep your last sleep.
Worms will consume your pride
the day you come tumbling.

You may write me off frauds
with the tips of your pens
and wipe all my traces
with your spittle and lies
since my style sickens you.
You may drag me through dung
to build your empire
on the bones of kinsmen
and tread the world bloated
but my songs will live on.
They will prick and plague you
just like light and conscience
if you fail to wake up
before the sun goes down.
They will grind your thinking
like a mill grinding corn
if you refuse to turn
before time wolfs your heart
and small minds will mock you
in the midst of mad dogs
in search of service stripes.
Wake up and stir the blood
of shameless little minds
prepared to kill to shine.
Wake up brother and sing,
wake up and sing with me
songs that sharpen the mind.

DO SOMETHING SANE

I write because I prize
the things that make me think
and act to make you see
the lies we strive to kill.
I write because I loathe
the things that make me cry,
things that make my heart beat,
things I know would for sure
make your thoughts wink an eye
and kiss kids in torn clothes.
Time will tolerate you
If you do something sane.

The wealthy do not care.
They only love to ride
on the backs of the poor.
They all love to listen
to music that cheers them,
music that bails bad blood
and shuts the door on love.
They do not think of death
drunk with lust and power,
blinded by greed and sloth.
The sawlike teeth of time
will saw the dolts to dust.

I write because I see
the things that hurt my heart
and rush my tongue to say
things that terrorise thieves

and make them waylay me.
I write because I feel
the pains of those who bleed,
those who spend their last days
eating dust and dry bread,
forced to sleep in thin sheets
in grey shacks without tops
even when time picks them.

You must do something sane
to outgrow the blind rage
and the crablike hatred
that choke your reasoning.
Do something that can last
before the eyes of sky
dim and darkness descends
sealing your piteous fate.
Write verses with punches,
not songs in praise garments
to have space in the ground
when time breaks your backbone.

SMALL MINDS

Small minds make a showcase
of their learning by rote.
They keep their minds on gain
and breathe down our lean necks
but cannot call to mind
the long and weary nights
we spent in chilly rooms,
waiting to be made out.
They are as treacherous
as a seasonal brook
and uninformed about
the iron teeth of time.

Small minds mint malevolence
mad keen about call girls
who rip their fans to shreds
and shut their ears to brains
striving to call to mind
the history of our land.
They bite like rattlesnakes
and rub salt in our wounds.
Their minds often go blank
when earth-shaking tasks sprout
and violent winds threaten
their shaky foundations.

I do not want to snap
like a tree in the storm
or wilt like heads of grain
though I can no longer

break up obstinate soil.
Like a chameleon's skin
that turns green on verdure
and becomes brown on dust
to assist it pull through
terrain fraught with risks,
I will change my garments
to fight shy of small minds.
My length of life and lore
have the right to walk out
head high, on little minds
that love to see the tears
and the blood of the mauled
drip,drip like rain water.
I have the right to slash
the tongues of little minds
that shed tears like crocodiles
when they want to wolf victims
just like the steel teeth of time
have the right to grind mankind.

GROOM OUR IMAGE

Though time tears my flesh
I walk as I talk
and talk as I think
though little minds think
I am old and done.
The smell of flowers
and the songs of trees
stooping to the wind
still give me pleasure.
My mind is still spry
burning up the miles
to lay bare our wounds
and fight corruption
to groom our image.

Though time gnaws your bones
you slant your speech still
and walk as Judas
though petty minds think
you are great and blunt.
The fate of the poor
and the tears of gloom
coursing down their cheeks
make you hug yourself.
You think like a child
and walk as a drunk,
your senses dried up
like sun-baked terrain
hostile and treeless.

You must understand that
time gives no second chance.
Our children need the truth
about where we come from
and where we are heading
just as crops need sunshine
and rain to grow mature
and bring forth bulky yields.
Our offspring need the truth
to grow strong and honest
to make our lives better
even when time grinds us.
They need uncontrived talk
and hearts emptied of tribe
to wipe clean our image,
yes, groom our soiled image
and dry the sap of vice
out of our people's blood
before time cuts us off
and vultures pick our eyes.

I WILL DO MY BEST

What cannot be knocked into shape
or smoked out like dry season bees
must either be left high and dry
or cut to the bone to kick back.
I have seen people come so close
to the threshold of destruction
because haughtiness closed their eyes
to as clear as day facts of life.
No one of fair and square feeling
would approve a mind that pretends
not to see the tears of the doomed
and the pus from their chronic sores
flowing like a stream close to us.

Small minds have often attacked me
since I started beating the drum
with some skill and stiff upper lip
calling my less travelled kinsmen
to join me in the hall of mores,
waiting for time to sort things out.
They still unleash storms of strictures
to keep learners away from me
and put to flight my doggedness.
I will do my best though ageing
to beat down my sly adversaries
for the seed of soundness to sprout
in my people's inmost being.

What cannot be imbued with sense
or harnessed like an untamed horse

must either be thrown overboard
or tied hand and foot and buried
for us to break with tribal fans
enriched through bribery and dodges.
I have seen people pervert truth
and mow down honest citizens
to cure their badly bruised egos
passing themselves off as patriots.
No one of right and proper taste
would dine with such bad character
nor join the rude ruling elite
to bleed our dear motherland dry.
I know I shall peg out someday
somewhere during my hard journey
worn out from howling my eyes out
for justice to wipe dry your tears.
I will do my best though ageing
to help you smoke out little minds
for the country to bloom and thrive
before time tears down everything.

KEEPING DISTANCE TO MOULD

My strong as a horse dream
to scale down the distance
between rich and poor folks
has been made away with.
I feel the firm fingers
of dark grim memories
claw the wounds in my heart.
How I wish I had wings
like a pitch-black swallow
I would be on the wing,
I would fly far away
to the calm of the sands,
keeping distance to mould
before I bite the dust.

I accept fate's verdict
my heart filled with protest
and would lie down till night
when the moon with white light
shines me into her stay.
I will not please the crowd
nor put up with smear dons
whose words are like honey
but in their hearts is hate.
They always twist my lines
to fill up their egos
and soothe their grand master.
I will keep clear of them
to give birth to cute poems.

The stars clad in light gowns
cry with loud bitter wails
but time strides on at ease.
Fruit trees have been stripped bare
and I have pains sleeping,
slit by the claws of time.
Worms feed on corrupt flesh,
fools maunder and mumble
and hearts as hard as rock
strip their hands to the bone
to protect their stomachs
and unearned positions.
I will distance myself
from them to mould my dream.

Though my dream has been soiled
in the front room of greed
and little minds rejoice
set on their bloody feet
by leaders without goals,
leaders with feet of clay,
run-of-the-mill leaders,
I will not plan evil.
I will keep my distance
to give my dream a wash.
I will stay at my post
where the day-star rises
and throw my spear at scabs
to show my true-blue pluck.

YEARS GONE BY

I yearn for the years gone by
when innocence was my mate,
when mother fed us with milk
and the ground was wet with love,
not with the blood of the poor
nor the bones of the weak-kneed
but with the cereals of life.

I yearn for the years gone by
and wish the eye of heaven
and the fury of lightning
could consign to raging flames
the filth of this vile epoch
and break the ribs of deceit
to plant peace and acquity.

The bad blood of youth is gone
and my heart pounds as I think
of the worms and the maggots
in the flesh of my people,
the corrupt flesh of my flesh.

I will not handcuff my tongue
nor tie conscience hand and foot
when thievery breeds havoc
and forgers fake to flourish.
I will not hold back my tongue
though my life is receding
and mediocrity gains ground.
I will refresh dying hearts

before the cord of life snaps.

I yearn for the years gone by
though my silvery hair mocks me
and the wind whistles outside
wildly wild with transient life.
Youths groomed for nation building
can fan to red-hot rancour
the feelings of the oppressed.
They can launch into the dark
to switch on social light bulbs.
I wish I were young and strong
to fight it out with con men
and dare mediocre leaders
to forfeit their positions
for the country to blossom.

SPITEFUL CONSCIENCE

The cutting words of the strong
and the fangs of the wicked
drive the wanting to violence.
Hurricanes cut and tear out
the hearts of trees and infants,
sometimes in the light of day
sometimes in the dead of night
year in year out at leisure
but the heartless do not care.
The wanting cannot withstand
the unbridled rage of storms
nor the bayonet-like tongues
of consciences full of spite.

In the nightmare of the dark
filled with bloodcurdling creatures
leagued with spiteful consciences
darkened by amoral jinns,
the strong and the dominant,
the wicked and the selfish
sequestered in their rancour
teach their young how to murder.
They wear their wrongs on their sleeves,
souls with spiteful consciences
and lay eggs of destruction
in the wounds of the limping,
ready to feast on their hearts.

I dare them, the dirty dogs
though I am a poor old man.

I dare them to pull the plug
on their out of kilter schemes
and free the soft in the head
from the claws of indigence.
Let them pass their full fingers
across the blistered temples
of peasants battling with death
at the peak of dry weather
and taste the taste of their wrongs.
Let them grieve for the oppressed
crying out beneath the wrongs
done to them without remorse
if not they will waste away
and splinter like rotting wood.
I dare you to stone to death
all consciences full of spite,
seeded with envy and strife
otherwise time will thrash you
and inearth your lust for fame.

TIRED AND SICK

Backscratchers turn one's head,
sail under false colours
and deceive the naive
into hawking their rights
for stale morsels of bread.
They tell their lies smoothly,
clip the wings of fond hope
and place before born fools
the dish that will kill them
in the heat of their lust.

I am tired of them
lifters of public funds
and the dishonest crowd
that always votes for them.
Their open wickedness
and slanderous discourse
have ground to bits my pride
and strong-armed impatience
into hassling my heart
as I always bark back.
Their dream for long has been
to take me by the throat.

Sometimes the pilferers
smile with bones in their mouths
and scoff contemptuously
when arraigned on charges
ranging from ritual rape
to murder and treason.

I wish you could join me
and share my awesome dreams,
my world and my passions,
my worries and my thrills
before I sag and sink.
I wish I could free you
from the prison of fear
and ask doves and leopards
to wrestle with bent brains
till new rules of conduct
take root in our country
and I leave the stage full.
I am tired and sick
of sharks and Judases
pilfering public funds
to fill our homes with gloom.

MOKOLO ELOBI

I know so well this part of town,
the shapes and sizes of the shacks,
the men and women who live here
breeding like rats year in year out,
battling with giant mosquitoes
around the clock with their bare hands.
The blood on their flea-ridden walls
reminds them of a prolonged war.

I know the ring road to their homes,
the risky short cut to their hearts,
the gutters and pools of urine
teeming with maggots fat like mice.
In the shelter of my deep thoughts
I hear a sustained piercing cry
break the deathly hush of the night,
the weight of its pain over me.

Often Mokolo Elobi
with her tentacles of garbage
and the waiting claws of decay
strike a jarring note in my head
urging me to thrust a sharp pen
into the heart of their anguish.
I have a thousand and one times
done their bidding prepared to die.

Before the cutting teeth of time
cut my intellect to the bone,
I must make politicians feel

the misery, the deadly wounds
and the sharp teeth of mosquitoes
biting deep into the spent flesh
of ditched Mokolo Elobi.
I must make the powers that be
get a whiff of the people's plight
and declare a war on negligence.
I must sing a militant song,
pull the plug on propaganda
and open fire on the beasts
breeding indifference to hardship
before the teeth of time tear me.
I will keep you at a distance,
you who call yourselves soul menders
if you fail in your great calling
to kiss Mokolo Elobi
before intolerant time strikes.

THE FACE I WANT

They crawl into my dreams
from the West like lizards
lean and longing for bread,
those who kissed hope goodbye
and went away from home,
far far away from home.
I respect their strength of mind
and count on them in return
to honour my stand in life
at least now that I am ripe
and like ripened banana
should be consumed with relish.

They creep into my dreams
from the East like leeches
limp and lost in dark thoughts,
those who gave up on hope
and went in search of fame,
far far away from home.
I take off my hat to them
in contempt of my grey age
and would expect them also
to respect my train of thought
though they have walked out on us
and worked out their way to thrive.

They sneak into my dreams
and linger in my mind
to move me move like them
away from home to gloom.

Time after time they come
beating drums dry as dust
in the bosom of the night
to force me to follow them.
I do not understand why
they return to haunt my sleep
when I have made known to them
the face I want to preserve
in the cupboard of history
alive and kicking or dead.
I do not want to be dragged
down the path of treachery.
I want to vet with my verse
the hardship of the masses
and the ease of the well-heeled
to reshape my country's face,
the face I want while alive
the right face that will save face
and keep me a safe distance
from injustice and mischief.

RUNNING WITH PATIENCE

I am still running the race
patient to reach the last lap
leaving behind a sick world.
I love my country though stained
by the blood of palm-greasing.
I am old and grey like ash
but I still feel the fresh hands
of my youth in my thin blood.

Coconut trees and my me
would soon be brown and barren.
The soil consumed with passion
and a craving for a drink
will quarrel with the day-star.
The dry season has been long,
too long for the earth's liking
but I keep running the race
hopeful of reaching the end
with an uncluttered conscience.
Though hatred and bitterness
grow in your heart like creepers
and lies sprout faster than truth,
I will keep running, sanguine
though preconceptions and spite
sink their claws into my flesh.

I am still running the race
serene though burning, burning
in the fires of slander.
If I could swing round the years

and speak in a different tongue,
intellectual chains will snap
like toothpicks and fly about
cutting and tearing traitors.

HEAVY HANDED

You have a weakness for dancing
to the rhythm of sheer power
while we your descendants languish
in the dungeon of indigence.
We bundle up corpses each day
in transparent plastic wrappings
and dispatch them in swift waters,
exhausted by always digging
and burying sterling talent.
Many of your choice associates
have fled the country crestfallen,
unable to dialogue with you.

I remember still the music
you have a soft spot for the most
whenever you wanted favour
and the number of times you danced
stark naked like an iguana
to the music of praise singers,
not thinking about our future.
We shall never harvest in peace
the coffee we cultivated
when foul fate brought us together
in the wake of independence
unless you reach your heavy hand
to your brothers battling for posts
in the backyard of deception.

Many of your close companions
have left the country in shambles

and with hearts heavy as concrete.
Your machiavellian style of life
darkened their world with hopelessness.
They felt with reason, they were born
on the wrong side of the blanket.
You and your newborn associates
took the sting out of their vision
and cursed them uphill and down dale.
They spent insomniac nights thinking
about the dawning of their day
or running from a volcano.
Their dreams of dwelling in sleek homes
with bondservants and chroniclers
fizzled out and were blown away.

CONTEMPTUOUS

I have opposed you since birth,
thrown your cord to mountain dogs
and clenched my biceps to rise
above the tides of your hate
for you and I selfish soul
to leave a mark on history.
You have consistently lied
and closed the door on dialogue.

I have scorned your shady deals
and run through the mass of mess
piled in the court of falsehood.
I feel the keen edge of loss
cutting through my tender heart
urging me to mend my views
since you left us in the dark
for space in the land of hope.

I am filled with contempt for you
and regret my ways with no tears,
fondling crazy thoughts of treason
for a rare name under the sun.
Have you no regrets countrymen
since you took to killing maggots

to save our arcane fatherland
since our brothers left overnight
for room in the house of freedom?
Have you any pangs of conscience
soldiers of the right struggling hard

to defend our dear motherland
since our brothers left disgusted?
There is prolonged tearing of hair
in homes where the only taper
has gone out, giving birth to fear.
Let us not allow our blood sweat
under the weight of little minds
else time will elbow us aside,
contemptuous of our abortion.

DEPLOY YOUR BRAINS

Do not sit in fear and trembling
for fear does not make things happen.
Those who have moved away from us
to carve a statue of their own
are mere mortals like you and I.
We can carve our own monument
from the mosaic of cultures
beckoning us to embrace them
to stand tall in a depraved world.
Deploy your brains my countrymen
for little minds to keep quiet.

Do not sit in fear and trembling
for fear does not make people see
the bloodstained sword of Damocles
hanging over them by a thread.
Do not fear my dear countrymen
for fear wrecks the essence of life
and consumes the liver of love.
We can erect our own museum
from the lore of our ancestors
obliging the rest of the world
to come in and kill their bias.

I promise to lie low for now
so that you can brandish your brains
determined to start life anew
in the absence of your brothers.
I promise to lie low for once
so that they can fill their pockets

and return to add to our lore
and paint the museum we erect.
If you fear, do so without tears
set to face political beasts
grown beefy on your ignorance.
Do not be afraid countrymen
for fear will not make us survive.
I know scores of you lust after
things that put the body at ease
and warm the cockles of the heart,
things that fill space in the stomach
but choke to death reason and self.
deploy your brains my countrymen
to take by storm oppressive minds
for the world to understand that
we can turn the face of the world.

ON THE VERGE OF SIXTY

In the shade of a tree
on the verge of sixty,
I look back in wonder
and remember the days
I walked the dusty streets
of Great Soppo barefoot,
gaunt and filthy dirty
in the heat of the sun.
I was over the moon
though in the arms of dread
screaming like a baby
in need of mother's milk.
My sharp screams sometimes drew
the wrath of lonely souls
searching where to lie down
and sing their blood dirges.
I do still remember
how from Esu I came
in the rawness of night
at two almost naked
my nostrils dripping wet.
I was ebullient then
in the shade of my mum
in the heat of dad's rage
but waiting to be fed
like a newly hatched bird.
My life was butter then
until I turned thirteen.
I began to feel deep
the teeth of existence

and the claws of jealousy
in a polygamous home.

I sneaked out everyday
as soon as I returned
from school hungry and dry,
in my mother's absence
to search fruit trees nearby
for something to fill me.
I saw deep deep rivers
rushing fast like the wind
and very high mountains
higher than Mount Fako
but I did not give up.
When thugs surrounded me
like werewolves in the dark
I pleaded with the gods,
summoned courage and glided
into the darkness of search.

On the verge of sixty
I still breathe and study
the ways and thoughts of man.
The winding ways of youth
have gone into thin air
but the god-awful scar
on the tip of my nose
and the danger ahead
lurking in the shadows,
make my blood run amok.
I cannot climb trees now
or walk the night with ease

as I used to do young.
When you see me thoughtful
on the threshold of sixty
do not think I have run short.

COME OUT

As I look down the years
once so filled with laughter
but so bleak and bare now
since my mates joined the foe,
I feel bald without them.

I have beaten the drum
we were brought up to beat
in front of the whole tribe
in times of deep deep pain.
I have danced the war dance
we were taught to enact
but I feel empty still.

As I look down the years
once so fresh and fragrant
but so dry and foul now
since greed gripped my soulmates,
I feel hollow and lost.

I have seen them glower
in a room filled with gold
and felt their boiling rage
in my spent heart and blood,
near the old bamboo hut
where we shared our secrets
but they look barren still.

Though it is pitch dark now
I still am filled with hope

waiting at the groundwork
where we learnt to keep watch
at the door of our lore.

There is still much time mates
before lightning comes down
and tragedy strikes hard.
I pray you should come out
from that dark room of shame
with incense of self-worth
not reek and beds of nails.

Come out from those people
who for a long time now
have grabbed and stashed away
in countries miles from home
our gold bars and diamonds.
Come out from their prison
where for many years now
you have slaved without gain
your psyche back to the wall,
struggling with loneliness.
If your sense of wrong dies
I will back you for life.

EMPATHY

When you intimate that
I hum throughout the day
like bees in the morning
and sit quiet in thought
like a loaf of stale bread,
I empathise with you.
You surely do not know
I listen to myself
to see things distinctly.
Do not think I am dull
or afraid to shoot you
with my old catapult.

When you see me head down
in the heart of the day,
do not think I am done
or afraid to stand up
like a soldier and face
the bullets in your voice.
You believe as usual
I do not deserve life.
You think you will not crack
when hailstones of the end
begin to drip and fall
cold, without sympathy.

If you think I have sagged
like a sack of white beans,
stop and watch how I drudge
day in day out shameless,

without gloves without props
in my remote spent farm.
I sympathise with you
whiling away your time,
chattering all day long
like an ace prostitute.
I feel sorry for you
loafing around, eating
what you never seeded.
At your declining age
you ought to have produced
something to feed the mind
and move the young to fight
the fight we could not fight.

COCKS NO LONGER CROW

There is heartbreaking weeping
and misery dances head high
in Esu my place of birth.
Death and hunger make merry
and sickness like night bandits
crawls from homestead to homestead.
The living and the dying
are too weak to resist them.

The daystar hardly comes out
and clockbirds have taken flight.
The thirsty earth is angry
piercing the feet of weaklings.
Peacocks no more raise their heads
and cocks do no longer crow.
The moon refuses to shine
and photographs of the dead
keep banging their knifelike fists
on the backbone of my brain.

The stricken and the grieving
the pain of my flesh and blood
stitch holes inside my inside.
They are like brown ants ready
to break in all directions
when kerosene touches them
but not sure of their morrow
like my people in the dark.
I hear change is on the way
though time preys on my body.

I know I will no more laugh
on the wrong side of my face.

RAGE IN HANDCUFFS

My heart in the grassland region
reaches out in fear and trembling
to kindle the hearts of people
strong in character and in love
with hearts that clasp hands with justice.
The cry of souls treated like dogs
is the cry of rage in handcuffs,
the cry the underdog blurts out
from the abyss of frustration
in frustration and agony.

The red eyes of the neglected
is the cry of limitless pain,
the pain genuine sons and daughters
of this strange triangle of ours
utter in the grip of mad minds
in the school of Machiavelli.
Neglect can drive some people mad
and the urge to be recognised
rent in the recesses of spite
can force people into exile.

My heart in the forest region
yearns for the death of jealousy,
blinding bloodthirsty jealousy
walking the streets unmolested,
dressed in ostentatious garments.
I remember a casual friend
drinking the cup of jealousy
at barely twenty and seven

in the cloudy forest of love
and my me wants jealousy dead.
Nothing can wake my casual friend,
nothing, from the sleep of envy.
I do not want to spill the beans
about your love affair with beasts,
I just have to bite the bulle

POISON IN MY BLOOD

Caught in the net of my thoughts
I see men dressed in old clothes
and women sick with the past.
I see children mad with rage,
their future chained in the dark
while grey dogs, senile and blind
crush the laps of the nation.
They spit on their people's pride,
the people that gave them votes.
They screw their eyes on Europe
and sing without shame their wish
to remain in the back seat
hoping to live till Christ comes.

Tyrants are flesh and blood too
but unlike bold as brass bards,
they cannot feel the heart's pulse
nor the heat of the oppressed.
Their breath is like rotten eggs
when clipping the wings of poets,
their wickedness like doped hounds
when tearing the hearts of foes.
I light my pipe in darkness
waiting for the Muse to rise
above the roof of my thoughts,
waiting for Time's bugle call
to give my songs eagle wings.

I think to live without dreams
makes life as it were, dizzy.

When traitors beat dark false drums
in the courts of the wealthy
who in league with violent men
kill the dreams of young artists,
I feel sick with frustration.
You may think I am bitter
because of my worn out age.
The treason in your squint eyes
and the demon in your voice
have lit anger in my heart
and put poison in my blood.

HEART IN BLACK

The days fly past quickly
garbed in morals and wit
yet no real change appears.
There are no stars in the sky
nor candles in my mud room,
only a rent heart in black
trying and trying again
to remove his morning clothes.

Boring months come and go
leaving slashes and shame
wrapped in perfumed plastic.
There is no freedom in sight
nor palm wine in my thatched house,
only a sad heart in tears
struggling to understand why
life gives more bricks than bouquets.

Years have come and vanished
dressed in beauty and hope
yet no genuine change comes.
There are no blooms in the yard
nor plum trees in the garden,
only a racked heart in pain
making an all-out effort
to change the music of grief.

I feel my people's pain
and share their bare life.
Though the sky is cloudy

and the storms of want scare,
I will not quit the land
for Europe's harsh landscape
nor vamoose to the U.S.
to become a brand new wreck,
ignored like a broken pot.
I do not want to huddle
at my hoary-headed age,
against unsafe foreign rocks
for want of a sleeping place.
I will irrigate my dreams
and crack jokes with pale silence
though my country is scabious
and I am in mourning clothes.
Though reduced to skin and bones
and poverty stalks the land,
I will continue to sing
against abuse and brute force
like a widow bent with grief
in the teeth of deprivation
while politicians feign fullness.

LEARNED MEN IN GREY

Our learned men in grey
have closed their cocky eyes
to the faeces round them
full of themselves like hawks.
The wind warbles death songs
as the days come and go
but they do not bother.

I see them counting francs,
our learned men in grey
in the heart of tombstones,
their heads bowed in worship
as though to be unctuous,
devoid of mercy were
the greatest arms to own.

The weather makes me sick
and the sky is graceless.
The moon no longer smiles
for full of promise youths
to dash forward and dance
a new face saving dance,
a dance to win over
young men of other states
to stop brains leaving home
for cold complex Europe.
Our learned men in grey
bury their heads in wine.
They are like vinegar
that sets the teeth on edge.

Sometimes luck smiles on them,
those who leave home for bread
and fame in far-flung lands
but often large numbers
go steady with hard drugs
not able to embrace
the dreams they left home for.
Our learned men in grey
have closed their bought off minds
to the woes of the doomed
in the throes of wreckage
in the land of free rein.
Our learned men in grey
cannot break through the clouds
nor set the clock backward
to correct their mistakes
and flash a smile before
they are cut down to size
and blown away like chaff.
They are not brave enough
to perish on their feet.

IGNOMINY

Since Sam arrived his new home
in the heart of thick Texas
in the choice year two thousand,
at the ripe age of sixty
with a degree in pure Maths,
I hear he just got employed.

He shines corpses in the day
and guards the senile at night,
a job he could not accept
while here with us living well.
I hear he wastes with regret
not able to feed his house.

He has sought to court suicide
many times on his weak knees
to put to death his ordeal.
The thought of his loving wife
and young children kill his dream.
The shame of coming back home
with no laurels nor hard cash
play hell with his last leaning
cocaine trade to feed his home.
The sweetness he longed to taste
and the scorn for his country
spurn the wreck of his body.

STATUS QUO

I had a myriad of dreams
as I grew taller and strong
unversed in bluff and tell tales,
bearing that breeds strife and war.
None of my dreams possessed wings
to fly out from my country
rich although raped day and night
in an attempt to wreck her.

I thought my playmates and I
would grow and form an army,
a great army to keep watch
at the gate of righteous rule
to shoot down rogues and rascals.
Tin gods and their hungry dogs
thumbscrews of the human race
like an arrow from the blue
came to power whips in hand
waving the big stick at us.
Time will give them nasty bites
and ditch them at any time.

Power has not changed since then
though the world is shifting fast.
Afraid to die dry, my friends
break free to seek pastures new
in lands supposed to be free
before their end pins them down.
I will go on living here
in this part of the country

where to think little of rule
can send you behind the bars.
I will not dog shallow wits
to sink in a foreign land.

NIGHTMARE OF LIFE

The nightmare of life in the West
does not freeze the blood of gamblers
packed like sardine in stained ships
old as the hills, bound for Europe.
They prefer unknown surroundings
to an old bare environment.

The terror of the night and sea
riding day and night with the mice,
dreaming of safe hands and good jobs
does not blow out the steady flame
burning bright in the stout steeled minds.
They see new life in the distance.

Left behind we piece our wild thoughts
and look for where to settle in
without the thorns of dread and tears
nor the sting of scorpions and bees.
We have one comfort left, the state
though she groans and bleeds in darkness.
We have to show her some respect
and take a serious stand for her
to burn the rubbish in her laps
and clean the blood of fallen friends
to break the sword of Damocles
and change the music of our lives.

CONTENT WITH MY ME

I am content with my me,
having drunk life at least
these many stone and red years
on a journey whose last stop
I cannot frame in my mind
because my me is finite.

I know that someday my me,
having trekked this rocky road
these many years of dreams lost
head high and chest thrust forward
like a king in his mansion
would lose its body and speech.

Only God my gas mask knows
the right station and the time
when my me shall pass away
and rest in its final stop.
Having watched the moon these years
rise and light up in season
sometimes with a cock-eyed smile,
sometimes with thrill on her face,
I know new flowers would grow
when death cuts down the wicked,
the vipers that have for years
dispatched thousands to their graves.

I am content with my me
watching through my eyes' window
the radiant rays of the sun

caress the boughs of fruit trees
in the freshness of the morn,
I feel full my nakedness.
I am content with my me
ready to kiss and buck up
the weak in the head pilgrim.
The hope of his heart crouches,
morose in the cell of dafts
whose delight is to shoot poets.
I am content with my me
though time lashes out at me
with the fury of a flood.

STARTING POINT

When I could barely give tongue,
my dad pregnant with pipe dreams
with feet not touching the ground,
increased the sum of my teeth
to put on a red feather.
This was the real starting point
the first step of the journey
I was bound to embark on
on the back of the unknown
on a dry and windy month.
The day was about to sink
stung by my leaving home raw.
When the moon got out of bed,
I saw tears form in her eyes
but could not say why she wept.

My heart did beat on leaving
not for what was left behind
but for what lay lost to sight.
I was shaken though so young
to reason to love the flight
without wings fluffy and fair.
At an age with teeth and brain,
when most people hate their past,
my heart still hungers for home
though deep and rooted in town
trying hard to build a new home
and raze memories too sore.
If you are incensed with me
whether for right or for wrong

let my remains not shade tears.
They should be laid to repose
and rot in any good soil
in any place in the land
when my course comes to an end
in a world so full of self.

WRITE A NEW STORY

You who little patience had
the moment your tongue loosened,
today you can stand and watch
in silence that claws the mind.
Today you can sit and stare
with ashen hair and moustache
like a dumb, the dance pattern
of upstart praise singing poets
searching in vain the secret
of living out what we know
to write out a new story.

Once your mind was earth-shaking
thrashing about and bitter,
clouded by the voice of self
trembling in the balance, weak
as a newly born baby.
Today you can stand and watch
people throw arrows at you
as if you were a traitor
trying to tear apart hearts
that laugh and cry together,
yearning for a new story.

Your mates have left the country,
each with a heart smitten through
and a nose bruised and bleeding.
They have gone somewhere to find
balsam oil for their deep wounds
and water for their dry throats.

They have gone somewhere to learn
to speak a different language
and write a new life story
with eyes like the red of dawn
peopled with tried and true minds.

ALWAYS CALL TO MIND

I have learnt to forgive
and be patient with fools
even when they pierce me.
I have never till now
been stirred to shed tears
and write for my own name
though the day to day spite
of false poets tears my heart
and makes my two children
sit as silent as stone.

I have looked through your plot
and seen small minds at work.
My heart is set on edge
and I feel the pain pierce
through the peeping eyes of
the one and only dream
we have left in this life,
the breakthrough of our kids.
I know you know we are
the most torn to ribbons
because we speak the truth
and cut crooks down to size.

You cannot, friend of old,
close the eyes of my mind
nor stop me from telling
the story of my life.
Too much of piping down
or holding back the tongue

can make an ass of one.
Always call to mind that
much has gone up in smoke
since we cannot agree
to smash the head of strife.
Too much labour of love
can give rise to contempt
and make us eat faeces.

VARNISHED WITH THE SAME BRUSH

You have beyond my wildest dreams
stopped drinking the wine of disgrace
that made you focus upside down
the lives of true-blue citizens
when you were drunk and unbridled.
Though varnished with the same brush
you saw beauty in the ugly
and the ugly in the comely
when you were tipsy and wet.

You reflect the normal man now
psyched up to sacrifice your life
to lower the banner of shame,
unfurl the green flag of honour
and hoist it in public places
for time to judge your decision.
Now you understand what it means
to live in turmoil and conflict
varnished with the same brush like me
with no single person on earth,
not even any living thing
ready to pass over your guilt.

I will journey along with you
singing your ground-breaking resolve
and give up everything for you
for time to remember our feat.
I will bear the brunt of risking
my name and awesome profession
to make the world pay you respect.

I have steeled myself for the cross
and whetted the knife of courage
in the midst of spineless vassals.
We are varnished with the same brush
so must buckle on our armour
to go through fire and water
and go down with colours flying
when the winds wing their way uphill.

TWO VOICES

I have what it takes
to be cool and plain
as the nose on my face.
We speak with two voices
you and I blind brothers,
trembling in the balance
of sabre-rattling sharks.

The wind is at play
and the moon frolics
fishing for new playmates.
I have watched the moon rise,
felt the caressing hands
and the soft soothing voice
of the wind thrill my heart
these many sundry years
yet you hug hatred still.

I envy the moon
and lust after her
ready for anything.
My heart has not grown old
though my hair is all white
like the white of an egg.
If I could hold my ground
like the moon every month,
I will stick at nothing
to goad those far from home
into growing their roots
dry in the diaspora
so we can speak one voice.

SEEKING A NEW IMAGE

Grief-stricken souls crowd your home
day to day to hear you sing
songs of a break in the clouds
hoping for the best to come.
They have their children at heart
but cannot rejoice with them
because they are far from home
kissing the hands of demons
to kill their hunger and thirst,
wearing long hair and make-up.

Give the poor people your heart
wrapped in your rose-coloured songs.
Give all those forlorn creatures
born under an evil star,
gathered in your home your love
covered in a dish with meat.
Their children in alien lands
fight not only the weather
but like yellow-eyed lovers
fly to arms to retain fame.
Some play a cat and mouse game
and keep well out of scandal.

Watching you pluck your guitar
singing about bleeding hearts
in and out of the country
makes me grow wild with delight
though your songs sometimes floor me.
I know you seek an image,

a new and forceful image,
the spitting image of home
not the death of your kinsmen
knocking themselves out for bread
in the country and abroad.
I am conscious that I must
wear my heart upon my sleeve
to grasp your saving grace songs.
and seek to see eye to eye
with tyrants and terrorists

MISCONSTRUED POET

Now that you cuddle your own pitch
after toiling long like a slave,
people from all domains of life
stop by your without paint abode
to salute a grey-haired singer
ready to rouse souls old and young.
Delinquents on the road to ruin
go past without breaking silence,
sickened and swollen with fury,
the fury of unmasked traitors.

The wind takes pleasure in your songs
and belts them out everywhere.
The birds of the air treasure them
and like the wind pipe them daily,
flitting from country to country
seeking for where to implant them
for people to mop their morals.
The moon is sometimes swathed in mist
and time hangs heavy on my hands
but the wind gives ear to your strains.

You work your fingers to the bone
and tire to death your senses,
looking for fitting words and tone
to sharpen our people's thinking
and present the sores of losers.
I make no bones about your art
and the fact that you need mettle
to write in rough weather and feuds.

I am the most misconstrued poet
the most slandered and derided
though my every word holds water.
Born out of wedlock lunatics
ready for anything, threaten
to cut off my name from the earth.
I have my temper by the throat.

TAKE OFF YOUR MASK

I cannot and will never
have a dig at my country.
I will praise her to the skies
but hold no brief for her sons.
I will take up arms for her
but launch out at her daughters.
I will shed my blood for her
but put to the sword her foes.

I cannot and will never
betray my exploited land
nor crush the spirit of work
to mend our broken fences
and make our country bear fruit.
I will cast the evil eye
on those who leave hold of her
and shake the dust from their feet
to dwell in faraway lands,
hoping to live better lives.

You cannot see with me now
but in the day of clean breasts,
you shall tell of the key role
we played grounding our people
before you fled the country.
On the leaves of my grieving,
the absence of your laughter
gnaws the spine of our culture
and the land, our land wriggles
like a worm in salt water.

You cannot see with me now
but in the day of naming
you shall give tongue to frankness
and take off your poaching mask
to declare we share one fate.

RISK OF RUST

There are no more patriots,
no more good life coaches
in this part of the world
where to think is to die.
The head of our culture
and the chest of our songs
are bare and on the rocks.
We run the risk of rout
since we no longer share
the same bout of sickness
nor speak the same language,
the dialect of slit hearts.

There is no more true love,
no more truth on our tongues
in this part of the land
where hearts are dead dry leaves.
The small voice of the poet
and the mouth of our pride
are at a loss for words.
We run the risk of rust
since we no longer cry
the same cry of hunger
nor dance the same dances,
the dances of dry hearts.

There is blood in your hands
though you puff like a toad.
I reach my trembling hand

to you my blood-stained friend
hoping you will sit up
and feel the bloody wounds
of those you came down on.
In the eyes of the world,
you are a great success
but remember miscreant,
we run the risk of rust
if you fail to sit up
when the drum of war beats.
I will run through your eyes
and History will clothe you
with linen lean and loose.

THERE WILL BE LIGHT AGAIN

The sky is still moonless tonight
and our children sigh in darkness.
There is no food for inventors
and fruit trees are without issue.
Fanatics are thorns in my flesh
and praise singers my tormentors.
Their voices rend the air, boiling
in the darkness of their hatred.

The sky is still starless tonight
and the artist sings in blackness.
The sirocco blows with fury
and hot dust settles on rooftops.
Naked children faint in the dust
and mendacious poets paint plenty.
I see a light in the distance
though haunted by your aversion.

The sky will be moonlit again
and the stars will shine starry-eyed.
Those who fled to other countries
will remember the part they played
canvassing support for new mores.
They will run over in their minds,
the fruitless battles for our rights
and the prolonged cry of anguish
gnawing with the teeth of anger
their way into our sore memories.
They will remember their cradle
and return ripe for fruitful frays.

There will be light again comrades
when the ugly and wrinkled face
of evil is besmeared with sores
and the bones of treason decay.

SHAMELESS SILENCE

Our dreams are often blown away
like dead leaves on a gusty day
and our days disappear like smoke
even in this part of the world
where people live in the future.
Sometimes the wealthy hire us
to lash life out of their soil
to make up for their deficit
and sustain the mouths in our homes,
clinging blindly to strange people.
The shameless silence of our folk
makes us take a gamble on life.

Our days are dribbled down the drain
like mucky and cheap plastic bags
and our wish for absorption melts
like flax that is burned with fire
even on this side of the globe
where government by the people counts.
The shameless silence of the land
sometimes drives us to dice with death
or waste ourselves fighting for crumbs,
in lands where we cannot prevail.
We are bent beneath our millstones,
worn out from thinking and hoping.

We have seen death cut down thousands
without a smile, without a sigh
in a country driven by self
and the virus of dominance

nipping in the bud challengers.
We left for Uncle Sam's country
having much to be thankful for
without looking on the bright side.
Wrapped up in the folly of pride
we left looking the other way
stung by the grandeur of the West.
We look back in remorse and shame
yet the shameless silence of mates
terrifies us out of our wits
and strangers scoff and shake their heads
to cut us off like heads of grain

BRED ON LORE

They ducked and ran because they feared
losing their heads in a storm nigh.
We stayed behind because we feared
losing our heads in desert sands
in lands to which we have no claim.
We stayed behind because we feared
breaking the neck of our country
for vultures to take advantage
and make short work of our values.
We are a people bred on lore,
ready to meet a sticky end
defending our ways and repute.

They left to be wealthy and free,
ready to sail too near the wind
looking forward to a green moon.
Our inner men were vexed to death
the day our brothers left for good
but we felt no hatred for them.
We knew they were going away
to chew the bones of obedience
and fill their insides with rubbish
or spill the blood of infringement
but we felt no grudge against them.
We are a people bred on lore,
ready to meet our Waterloo
for the survival of our ways.

The country misses them, the gone
and the land feels their betrayal.

We lift up our voices and weep
trusting God for new stars to rise
from the river tears of our grief
to pull the plug on two-faced minds.
It makes our hearts bleed very much
not so much because they have gone
but because the land is in bed.
We fear our ways would be swallowed
as the grave swallows its victims.
Only new and top-flight doctors
in honour bound can treat the land.
Only hearts with a clear conscience
and mouths in the line of duty
can put the country on her feet.

I CANNOT RESTRAIN MYSELF

Entreat me not to lament
the destiny of my friends
gone to sojourn in a land
where each celestial body
has talons and teeth of steel.
I cannot restrain myself
from thinking about their lot
and the bad blood in our land.

I hear an overwrought voice
calling for help in darkness,
blood gushing out of his wounds
like oil from a broken pipe.
I pick up his voice clearly
calling for relief in grief
like a wench in labour pains.
I cannot refrain myself
from talking about his plight
until I know he is loose.

Entreat me not to forget
the torments of my brothers
gone to reside in a land
where the daystar and the moon
emit light when they choose to.
The sad echoes of their stay
hit my eardrums hard and sharp
like drumbeats from expert hands.
You can now understand why
I cannot restrain myself

from writing about their pains
where they are lightly esteemed.

I DOFF MY CAP

Some of them got on well
when they came to full rest
and still make out their way
today sometimes worked up,
sometimes keeping their cool
when defamed and harassed.
They have not forgotten
the cute land of their birth
messed up by greed and graft
pleased with the sloppy rags
clinging to the frail frames
of folks on the breadline.

The hapless were ashamed
of their defiled beauty
but hoped their sun would rise
to scorch the leaves of death.
The fragments of their dreams
bleated day in day out
like a starved tethered goat
until a rage gripped them,
a rage that harassed them,
a rage that could even
give an angel headache.
They broke the bones of fear,
spat in the eyes of thugs
and heaped abuse on fate.

Coming back home was faint,
weakened by clouds of doubt

clothed in black and crimson.
They struggled to look through
the miasma of stern time
to work over their past
and decide how they can
thaw the snow around them.
The coldness in their bones
and the aching for life
drive them to fight to live
or peg out in silence
like mice and mosquitoes.
They have vowed not to die
without tracing new trails.
I doff my cap to them.

INCENSE OF HOME

I love the incense of home
and the contours of my land
though the flower of my age
begins to droop in the heat
like cut blooms without water.

The silence of leading brains
and the vagueness of some poets
cannot pull out the hard up
or lift those sunk in despair
from the stack of rotten eggs.

I love the bearing of home
and the beauty of my land
though the daytime of my life
begins to fade in the sun
like cloth washed in hot water.

The silence of lead statesmen
and the sang-froid of most youths
cannot snatch ill-fated goats
from the mouth of the lion.
I forget to eat my bread
and clean the mess around me
not because I am wilting
but because my country's heart
has been torn out by rascals
and given to dogs to chew.
I feel like blowing my top
watching thousands of people

live out their lives on their knees.
I feel the rage of the wind
in my spent hip and wrist bones.

SHROUDED IN MIST

Sometimes when the sun is spent,
I climb the roof of my life
to view my sick land better
and watch, my heart in my mouth
beggars beleaguer the streets
with blasting bowls of hunger.
Their sharp voices and sad songs
shake the walls of wicked souls,
leading their own flesh and blood
and the nation to be burnt.

The walls of wickedness shake
but do not crash to the ground
because the display of pride
and the brass neck of your heart
have cut the throat of your mind.
You no longer prop the poor
nor stand the hassling requests
and charges of their stomachs.
My soul is knit to their souls
though I am advanced in years.

The land is shrouded in mist
and the lowing of drained cows
echoes in my burdened mind.
The swelling pride of the rich
and the rubber stamp in love
lost in the thick mists of time,
make my shrunken muscles ache.
The sound of my groaning bones

fans the embers of nightfall
when most creatures go to sleep.
I try hard for Sleep to sprint
from the grounds of Morpheus
and beat time for me to sleep
though murk hangs over the land
and my days tick by at ease.

THE LAND LIES LIFELESS

How lifeless lies the land
now when the moon is full,
in times past full of verve.
How like a tramp she looks
she who in times gone by,
was the dream of all hands
and the pride of great minds.

She has been raped often
and her bloodstained bed creaks.
Mangled, she weeps at night
her once big round breasts flat,
she who in times gone by
was the first choice of all
and the sweetheart of poets.

Tears still run down her cheeks
and those who once loved her
have cast her off and fled.
No one is close at hand
to make her sleep pain off
and clear the ground for her
to grow new crops and blooms.
This is what makes me moan.
My wrinkled heart twitches
like a cat on hot bricks
as I look past my days
marked out by sacrifice.
Time will vindicate me
though little minds mock me.

BAD BLOOD

I cannot keep my tongue from speech
when evil that flesh is heir to
and people on the gravy train
defame without remorse my name.
I cannot bottle up my thoughts
or draw a veil over falsehood
when Iagos and death walk the streets
dressed like newly named ministers
and people wrapped up in themselves
clip the wings of my dignity.
I cannot keep my big mouth shut
when tribalism shakes our roots.

How do you expect a patriot
to neither confirm nor deny
the seeds of cruelty in our hearts
and the creepy-crawlies of death
setting us against each other?
How do you expect a highbrow
to put a bridle on his tongue
when children are undernourished
because bad blood flows in the land
and the load of bondage breaks us?
I cannot bed down with sealed lips
when my country is deep in graft.

Life is squeezed out of the feeble
who all their life time have laboured,
content to live and have a meal
like a cat with a dish of cream.

I cannot keep my tongue from speech
when bastards bat people like ping-pong
and death lingers over the land
I am fond of like my own soul.
I cannot keep my tongue from speech
when foes drive a wedge between us.
I cannot keep my big mouth shut
when deceptive tongues tap our blood
like tapping fresh trees for rubber
and bad blood disunites the land.
I cannot hold my mouthy mouth
when the roofs over our heads leak.

A NEW DAWN IN GESTATION

A new dawn is in gestation
in this part of the world, my world.
A new order would soon be born
in the world and in my country
disfigured by the fists of greed.
I see no cause for long faces
when the fields are covered with corn
and fruit trees are heavy with buds.
I see no cause for long faces
when the weather is behind us
to quench fires of oppression.

I can go away now happy
after a journey full of thorns.
I can go away now fulfilled
into the great belly of earth.
If I cross to the other side,
make sure you continue to love
each other as you love your souls
for the family name to shine.
If the canines of time tear me,
make sure you continue to hope
even when small minds molest you.

Surely a new dawn is around,
a new order would soon see light
in Africa, in the whole world.
I see no cause for depression
when the moon is about to rise
to break the power of darkness

and subject all owls to bondage.
Make sure our culture is not drowned
when I cross to the other side
for our clan to be acknowledged.
Men and women to take after
shall spring to the defence of truth
and pull down walls and fences
that divide and set souls at odds.
They shall be the drive and the heart
of talent when my breathing stops,
taking the wind out of your sails.
When the ripples of little minds
and the bitter bite of the wind
begin to wash over your mind,
threatening to blow you to bits,
think of a new dawn ripening.

www.ingramcontent.com/pod-product-compliance
Lightning Source LLC
Chambersburg PA
CBHW031637160426
43196CB00006B/452